Unlock the Power of Your Chromecast

(March 2014 Edition)

By Aaron J. Halbert

To receive FREE monthly updates to this book in Kindle and PDF format, subscribe to my mailing list. You can find the link on the last page of this book. I will not share your email address with anyone else!

To see what's new in this edition, look here (p.51).

Table of Contents

Foreword

Thank you very much for purchasing *Unlock the Power of Your Chromecast*. I have worked hard to compile only the most relevant and useful information for you, and I firmly believe that you will get your money's worth.

If you have any feedback on this book, please feel free to email me at AJH@AaronHalbert.com or post a review on Amazon. By doing so, you will help all Chromecast users get the information they need, and you will also have my enduring gratitude. I carefully read and consider all the comments I get, because I believe in listening to my customers.

In this book, I mention a few paid services that can help you get more out of your Chromecast. I want you to know that (1) I always mention free alternatives to paid options when they're available, and (2) I am not affiliated with any of the services I recommend in this book. All of my recommendations are completely objective and based on my own experience with my Chromecast. I will not receive any type of commission if you pay for services I recommend.

I also realize that because the Chromecast is only $35, it doesn't make sense to spend a lot of extra money to maximize your use of it. That's why I have tried to keep my recommendations of paid services to a bare minimum, and why I have priced this book at such a low price point.

Also, here's a tip: If you have already read a previous edition of this book, you'll want to take a look at the Appendix of Updates (p.51) to see what's changed.

Enjoy!

Introduction

If you just purchased a Chromecast or received one as a gift, this book is for you.

If you already have a Chromecast and you want to maximize its potential, this book is for you.

If you haven't yet bought a Chromecast, but you want to understand all of the amazing things you can do with it, this book is for you.

If you just plan to use your Chromecast for streaming Netflix and YouTube, and nothing else, you probably *don't* need this book. It's not that hard to plug in the Chromecast, configure it, and start streaming video.

But if that's all you plan to do, you're leaving a lot on the table. The Chromecast appears deceptively simple at first, but there are dozens of subtle, undocumented, and unknown features built into your Chromecast that you'll never know about without this book. And they're not just "fun" features for hackers and enthusiasts—many of them are very valuable for average, everyday use.

Since the Chromecast is already so cheap ($35 MSRP), I have priced this book at the lowest price possible. It's a small fraction of the Chromecast's cost, but it will help you unlock dozens of new features. You'll learn techniques that will save you hundreds of dollars on other products and services, like how to use your Chromecast with hotel TVs to avoid paying pay-per-view fees. This book will help you power up your $35 Chromecast to compete with more expensive alternatives like the Apple TV and Roku.

Better yet, this book is straight to the point. There are no long chapters to trudge through, and no extra words to waste your time. You'll be able to read this book in about one hour so you can start getting the most out of your Chromecast right away.

To take full advantage of the information in this book, you will need (1) a desktop or laptop computer running Windows or Mac OS, with Google Chrome and the Chromecast extension installed (p.11), (2) an iOS or Android phone or tablet, and (3) a wireless router with an active Internet connection. In writing this book, I have made the assumption that readers have all of these things.

So, without further delay, congratulations on your new Chromecast, and enjoy all of the excellent things you can do with it!

What Exactly Does the Chromecast Do?

Since you're reading this book, I assume you at least understand the Chromecast's basic purpose, which is to send Internet video to your TV. This is true, but there's more to the story.

The first thing to know is that the Chromecast can actually send audio and photos in addition to video. I will teach you all about this.

The second thing to know is that unlike rivals such as the Apple TV and the Roku, the Chromecast doesn't actually do anything by itself. The Apple TV and Roku have built-in content "channels" like Netflix and Hulu, and can directly play video from these channels without the help of any other device. They have regular remote controls and on-screen menus like your HDTV or DVR. In contrast, the Chromecast can only be used in conjunction with a phone, tablet, or computer, which "casts" audio or video to the Chromecast and acts as your both menu and remote control. If you aren't controlling the Chromecast with another device, it doesn't do anything except display a screensaver.

In fact, that's why it's called the Chromecast instead of the Chromestream—because when you start playing content on your Chromecast, what you are really doing is sending ("casting") it a link to the audio or video file on the Internet. The file itself doesn't actually stream *through* the device you cast with; rather, it goes directly from your wireless router to the Chromecast. This is actually a very important and helpful feature. Why? Because it frees up your phone, tablet, or computer for other tasks, and doesn't drain its CPU and battery power.

For example, if you use your smartphone to cast a YouTube video to your Chromecast, you don't have to leave the YouTube app open to keep playing the video. You can press your home screen button to leave the app, and then do anything else you please while your video continues to play. Very handy, and much better than using an HDMI cable that would require you to leave the song or video app open the whole time.

However, the Chromecast's focus on casting instead of streaming is also one of its biggest limitations: It doesn't have such great support for casting files saved on a hard disk. Although it is possible to do so, it requires third-party software and is not nearly as easy as casting content from the Internet. More on this later.

Right now, Google has official partnerships with the following services:

•Netflix

•HBO GO

•Hulu Plus

•Pandora

•YouTube

•Google Play TV & Movies

•Google Play Music

•VEVO

•Red Bull TV

•Songza

•Plex

•PostTV

•Viki

•RealPlayer Cloud

… and several other, smaller services.

When you play music or video using any of these services, whether it is on your computer or mobile device, the player interface will have a casting icon like this:

Clicking this icon will cast the audio or video to your Chromecast, and stop it playing on the device you are using.

You might have noticed some big names missing from Google's list of partners. Notable examples include iTunes, Disney's online video services, ESPN, MLB, NBA, major news channels like FOX and NBC, Amazon Instant Video, and so on. None of these services have a casting icon in their player, so you will not be able to directly cast them to your Chromecast. Fortunately, the Chromecast has two important features that can be used as workarounds for many of these missing content providers: casting web pages and casting your entire screen. (However, these features only work on Windows and Mac OS, not iOS or Android.)

Let's say that your cable package allows you to stream ESPN online. Although ESPN does not currently support casting to the Chromecast, you can simply cast the ESPN stream web page from the Chrome PC browser to your Chromecast as a workaround. Sometimes this method results in lower video quality than casting from Google's partners, but it is still very watchable, and has been greatly improved since the Chromecast first came out.

As for the full screen feature, "Great," you might think, "That's a workaround for casting iTunes and downloaded movies." Unfortunately, it's not quite that easy, and for a silly reason, too—casting your whole screen does not yet include audio. So if you cast a video playing in a program like Windows Media Player or QuickTime, the audio will play on your computer, not your HDTV. If you cast an audio file, nothing will be sent to your Chromecast at all except the screen's image.

Of course, as I promised earlier, there are workarounds. I will teach you exactly how to use these workarounds, along with all of the other features I have mentioned so far. By the end of this book, you will fully understand what you can and cannot do with your Chromecast.

To summarize, out of the box the Chromecast is only meant for playing audio and video from services included in the bulleted list, above. With this guide, not only will you be able to use those services, but you will also be able to cast any video on the Internet, as well as any photos, audio and video saved on your computer hard drive. I'll also show you some options for playing audio and video from your Android or iOS device, as well as provide many other tips and tricks for getting the most value out of your Chromecast.

Let's go!

First Things First: Setting Up Your Chromecast

Google makes it pretty easy to set up your Chromecast, so instead of repeating their instructions in exhaustive detail, I'll just give you a few pointers.

For the initial hardware setup, all you need to do is plug your Chromecast into a free HDMI port on your HDTV and plug in the power adapter. If your HDTV has a USB port, you can plug the Chromecast's USB cable into it instead of the wall plug, but I suggest using the wall plug. This is because (1) the wall plug is more reliable, and (2) for many newer HDTVs this will also allow you to use a neat feature whereby your Chromecast can power your TV on by itself (p.31). Also, be sure to use the cable that comes with the Chromecast. Not all micro USB cables are created equal, and low quality cables can cause big problems.

After you have connected your Chromecast, change your HDTV's input to the Chromecast's HDMI port and then point your computer's browser to http://google.com/chromecast/setup. Download the setup app and run it. Note that your computer must have Wi-Fi capability. Generally this will only be a problem if you have an older desktop PC. Most newer PCs and laptops have a Wi-Fi card built in.

If you do not have a computer or laptop with a Wi-Fi connection, you can use an iOS or Android device instead; just go to the above website on your mobile browser and download the Chromecast mobile setup app. I suggest, however, using a Windows or Mac OS computer if possible. I have found the desktop setup software to be more reliable than the mobile software.

If you get lost anywhere along the way, consult the following website for step-by-step installation instructions: https://support.google.com/chromecast/answer/2998341?hl=en&ref_topic =3058948

Most of you will not have any problems setting up your Chromecast for the first time, but if you do, Google has kindly set up a troubleshooting site. If necessary, access it here: https://support.google.com/chromecast/troubleshooter/2995236

Google also has an official Chromecast support forum where you can ask for help: https://productforums.google.com/forum/#!forum/chromecast

After you have successfully configured your Chromecast, install the Chrome web browser on your desktop or laptop computer if you don't already have it. https://www.google.com/intl/en/chrome/browser/

Then, download and install the Google Cast extension in Chrome. It's different than the setup utility, and you'll need it for a lot of the techniques in this book. https://chrome.google.com/webstore/detail/google-cast/boadgeojelhgndaghljhdicfkmllpafd?hl=en

Casting from Chromecast "Apps": The Easiest Way to Cast Video

The video providers that have partnered with Google to offer a built-in Chromecast button are called Chromecast "Apps." By far, these are the easiest services to cast using your Chromecast, because casting support is built into all of them, and you do not need to use workarounds like casting from a Chrome browser tab.

When using a desktop or laptop, you just go to the service provider's website (e.g., Netflix.com or YouTube.com) using the Google Chrome web browser with the Google Cast extension installed, and click the Cast icon, which you'll find near the play button.

As I noted in the section, What Exactly Does the Chromecast Do? (p.8), as of March 2014 official Chromecast Apps include the following:

•Netflix

•HBO GO

•Hulu Plus

•Pandora

•YouTube

•Google Play TV & Movies

•Google Play Music

•VEVO

•Red Bull TV

•Songza

•Plex

•PostTV

•Viki

•RealPlayer Cloud

… and several other, smaller services.

However, Google's use of the term "App" is kind of confusing in this context. Usually we think of apps as programs you download for smartphones and tablets, but Google's use of "App" is different in this case.

A Chromecast "App" simply means any of the above video providers that have built-in Chromecast functionality. So, it calls Netflix, YouTube, and so on, "Apps." You and I would probably use the term "websites" instead. There is no program to download when using a Chromecast "App." To use a Chromecast "App" like Netflix or YouTube, you just go to its website as you normally would, and click the Cast button.

Seems unnecessarily confusing, doesn't it?

To add to the confusion, if you cast from an iOS or Android mobile device rather than your desktop computer, you *will* actually initiate casting from the service provider's mobile app (the kind that you download from the Play Store or App Store), because directly casting from an app is the *only* way to cast video on a mobile device. (Since mobile Google Chrome does not support extensions, there is no way to install the Google Cast extension on an iOS or Android device. Therefore, you must rely solely on the casting functionality built in to the video providers' actual mobile apps.)

Whew! Anyway, the bottom line is that to cast audio or video from any of the services listed above, all you have to do is look for the Cast button. You'll find it in the media player interface, no matter which device you're using.

Casting All Other Online Videos Using Google Chrome Tabs

Now you know how to cast video from any of the video providers ("Apps") with which Google has partnered. But what if you want to watch a video from another content provider, like ESPN, a news channel, Vimeo, DailyMotion, etc.? You won't find a Cast icon in these providers' media players. So, instead, you will have to use Chrome's Google Cast extension to cast an entire tab.

To do this, open a new tab in Chrome and navigate to the video you wish to watch. Play the video. Click on the Google Cast button in the upper-right-hand corner of the Chrome window, and then the name of the Chromecast to which you wish to cast the video. (Sometimes your Chromecast will not appear in the list right away; if this happens, just click out of the menu and click on the Google Cast button again. Your Chromecast will appear in the menu.)

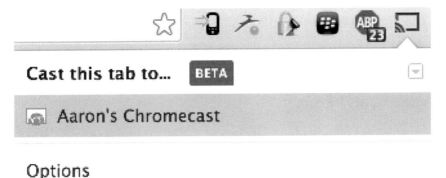

Wait until the video starts playing on your HDTV, and then make the video full-screen using the controls in the video player. That's it—you've casted a non-Chromecast App video.

If you want to continue to use your computer while the video casts in the background, follow these instructions.

•**Windows users**: Hold the ALT key and press Tab to select another program to open on top of the full-screen video. For example, you can open Chrome, and the full-screen video will continue to play in the background. The only problem with this approach is that if you go back to the Windows desktop, the video will continue to cover your taskbar and Start menu. If this is a problem, you can prevent it by using VirtuaWin, a free virtual desktop manager that will let you create a completely separate desktop to conduct your Chromecast business.
http://virtuawin.sourceforge.net/

•**Mac OS users**: Hold the Command key and press Tab until "Finder" is selected. The Dock will appear at the bottom of your screen. Right click on the Chrome icon and select "Hide." Your full-screen Chrome window will be hidden but continue to play on your Chromecast in the background. Unfortunately, unlike Windows, it is not possible to continue to browse on Chrome while a full-screen video is playing in the background. If you want to browse the Internet, you'll have to use another browser like Safari or Firefox. I know this is very annoying, but there is no fix available yet.

To return to your video at any time, just use Alt+Tab or Command+Tab again.

Casting Web Pages

You can also use this feature to cast a regular web page to your HDTV if you want to browse on the big screen. However, there's an annoying limitation—your mouse pointer won't be casted. If you're feeling adventurous, you can work around this limitation by installing an unofficial Chrome extension from the following link. Be warned, it's completely unofficial and may not work perfectly. I found that the pointer moved erratically with this extension, ultimately ending up in the right place but following a strange path along the way. Don't expect the moon from this extension. However, it's the only option right now if you want a mouse pointer.

http://www.reddit.com/r/Chromecast/comments/1k4kas/is_there_a_way_t o_have_chromecast_cast_the/cbo8i4y

Casting Your Entire Screen

If you want to cast your computer desktop, or programs that are not web pages, you can use the Chromecast's experimental screen casting feature. As I mentioned earlier, at first this may seem like a good way to cast iTunes content or other media saved on your computer, until you realize that screen casting does not support audio. (Don't worry, I'll show you how to get around this limitation in a moment.) (p.21) Also, the video frame rate is quite poor when using this method, so it won't even work for that Charlie Chaplin silent movie you've been dying to watch.

In that case, what is screen casting good for? Here are some ideas:

•Still photos saved on your hard drive on in a program like iPhoto

•PowerPoint presentations (the Chromecast is a lot easier to carry than a projector, assuming an HDTV is available for you to cast to)

•Any other **still content** you wish to display on a much larger screen

To enable screen casting, click the Google Cast button in Chrome, and then the tiny down arrow in the menu that appears. Click "Cast entire screen (experimental)." Don't get your hopes up about the "Audio mode" setting, because it does nothing even when selected. Finally, click your Chromecast's name and approve the casting request if prompted.

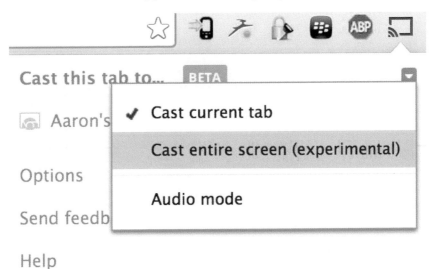

Screen casting needs some improvement, but even with its limitations it is a handy feature.

Casting Music, Pictures, and Video Saved on Your Hard Drive

The Drag-and-Drop Method

Do you have music, photos, or videos saved on your computer's hard disk? You can cast them using the Drag-and-Drop method as long as they are common file types such as MP4, MP3, 3GP, OGG, MKV, JPG, and so on. Unfortunately, many users have reported that they are unable to play AVI files, one notably common movie format. Some MKV files can cause also cause trouble depending on their encoding.

To try this technique, find the icon for your file and drag it into an open Chrome tab. (You can also enter **file:///** into the URL field of a Chrome tab, press Enter, and browse your hard drive that way.)

If it starts to play, you're set—just cast the tab. If it does not play, it is not in a format you can cast using this method.

If this happens, you still have some options. First, you can download free software to convert the file into a compatible format (I recommend Handbrake http://handbrake.fr/). If you use Handbrake, you'll want to convert any movie files into MP4 with AAC and X264, and any music files into MP3, which are the most compatible Chromecast formats. Alternatively, you can try a service called Plex, which I explain in the next section.

In my opinion, the drag-and-drop method is mostly useful for casting movies, because you can only cast one file at a time, which is bad for listening to songs or viewing photo albums. Fortunately, there are two good, free ways to cast your music (p.21) that I will teach you shortly. As for casting photos, I suggest you upload them to an online album such as Flick or Picasa, which you can then cast using the tab-casting method. That way, you can browse through the album properly, rather than dragging one file at a time from your hard drive into the Chrome window.

The main advantage of the Drag-and-Drop method is that it's totally free. If you're willing to spend a tiny bit of money to cast your media collection to your Chromecast, though, take a look at Plex.

Plex

You might have noticed a bizarrely named service, Plex, in the list of official Chromecast Apps. What is Plex, and why am I mentioning it now?

If dragging files into Chrome is the yellow taxi method of casting your saved media, Plex is the limousine. Plex actually does much more than cast video; it sets up a media server on your computer that allows you to stream your saved music, pictures, and video to any other computer, smartphone, or tablet, at any time over the Internet. For example, Plex allows you to view media saved on your computer, on any other computer that is connected to the Internet (e.g., at your friends' houses). Chromecast support is just one of the many ways of viewing saved media with Plex. It takes care of all video converting on the fly, so you don't have to worry about file compatibility, and has a Cast button for maximum ease of use. It even works with content purchased from iTunes.

There is a catch, however—for now, Chromecast support is part of the paid Plex Pass subscription program, which is priced from $3.99 monthly. Plex plans to make Chromecast support free at some unspecified point in the future, but no date has been announced yet.

I find Plex to be an excellent service and by far the best way to get your personal media collection on your Chromecast if you're not satisfied with the free Drag-and-Drop method. I have no affiliation with Plex and I will not profit if you sign up with them; I'm just telling you that it's the best option out there. There are no free services that can match Plex's Chromecast support.

You can learn more about Plex here. https://www.plex.tv/

Plex Mobile App

Available for both iOS and Android, the Plex Mobile App allows you to use your iOS or Android device to cast video, music, or photos from your Plex media server to your Chromecast. Essentially, it turns your mobile device into a remote control for Plex software already installed on your PC. Note that the Plex Mobile App does NOT cast video that is saved on your iOS or Android device itself. To do that, see this section (p.24).

As with the desktop version of Plex, casting is only possible if you have a Plex Pass subscription, which as I noted, starts from $3.99 per month.

The Plex mobile app is normally $4.99 for both iOS and Android, but if you have a Plex Pass subscription, you can download a special free version for subscribers instead. Look for it in the Google Play Store and the Apple App Store under "Plex for PlexPass."

If You Really Don't Want to Pay for Plex…

There are a couple ways to use Plex with your Chromecast without paying for a Plex Pass subscription. Be warned—these methods will save you money, but are unofficial and may not always work the way you expect. The easiest and most consistent way to cast your saved media on your Chromecast is to just pay the $3.99 monthly fee to Plex.

If you have an Android, you can set up the free Plex Media Server on your PC, download Avia from the Play Store, unlock Chromecast support for a one-time $2.99 fee, and use Avia to cast from your Plex library to your Chromecast. (If your Plex Media Server is properly set up and your Android is on the same Wi-Fi network, Avia will automatically detect the content on your Plex Media Server.) By doing this, you will not have to pay the $3.99 monthly fee for Plex Pass. The trade-off is that you get no official support, and the two programs may not always work together seamlessly.

Alternatively, you can install the free Plex Media Server on your PC and use its Media Manager feature to play your content in another Chrome tab on your PC. You can then cast that tab to your Chromecast using Google Cast's tab-casting feature. This method can be laggy and produce lower quality results than the Plex Pass Chromecast features, but it won't cost you anything.

Casting iTunes, Window Media Player, or Another Music Library

Using Sockso

If you manage your music collection in a program like iTunes or Windows Media Player, there is a way to cast it to your Chromecast. Since I have already explained that full screen casting is not the solution to this problem, how does one accomplish this?

The answer is a media web server. First, download Sockso and install it on your computer. http://sockso.pu-gh.com/

Open it, go to the "Collection" tab, and add the folders that contain your music collection.

Now, open Chrome and point it to this URL: http://127.0.0.1:4444/

In the upper-right-hand corner of the screen, you will see a drop-down menu prefixed with "Play using." Change this to "Embedded Flash Player."

Now, cast the tab, and play music to your heart's content. You can browse your library and create playlists just as you would in any other music player.

Note that Sockso does not have very good M4A support, so if you have a large library of M4A files, you may need to convert them to another format before casting them to your Chromecast. Sockso has good support for other major file types, including MP3 and WMA.

Using Google Music

If setting up Sockso sounds too complicated, or you don't like the idea of running a media server on your computer, you can upload your music collection to Google Music instead and then tab-cast it from Chrome. Google Music is a cloud music player that allows you to upload up to 20,000 songs for free, which can then be accessed from any computer or mobile device over the Internet.

The advantages of this method are (1) no additional software on your computer, and (2) you can use the Android Google Play Music app to control your music casting instead of having to sit down at your laptop or desktop computer. Also, you get the added bonus of having your music library available anywhere you have an Internet connection.

The main disadvantage of using Google Music is that it can take a long time to upload your collection. Also, you'll have to pay if you want to upload more than 20,000 songs.

To get started with Google Music, go here: http://music.google.com

Casting from Spotify and Grooveshark

Neither Spotify nor Grooveshark are official Chromecast Apps yet, but you can still cast from them. For Spotify, use the web player instead of the desktop software, and cast the tab. Grooveshark is purely online, so it's the same deal—just cast the tab.

There is not yet a way to cast Spotify or Grooveshark from an iOS or Android mobile device.

Casting Music, Pictures, and Video Saved on Your Mobile Device

We've already covered how to cast media saved on your computer's hard drive. But what if you want to cast media saved on your phone or tablet? It's pretty easy; just keep reading.

Keep in mind that casting saved media from your Android or iOS device will use more processor and battery power than apps like YouTube or Netflix that stream from the Internet. Remember how I explained that casting just means sending a link to the Chromecast, and that's good because it saves your device's resources? That doesn't apply when you cast saved media, because there is no link to send. Rather, your device has to keep working in the background to stream your file to your Chromecast. So, if you plan to stream saved media, keep an eye on your battery level and know that your other apps might slow down. That said, casting saved files shouldn't be a major drain, so don't let this warning get in the way of enjoying yourself!

Android

To cast media saved on your Android device, my recommendation is an app called Avia. It is capable of casting music, pictures, and video on your Android or its SD card—an all-in-one package. Avia is free to download from the Play Store, but requires a one-time in-app purchase of $2.99 to unlock Chromecast support. In my opinion, this one-time fee is well worth it.

A number of competitors to Avia have popped up in recent weeks, including AllCast, LocalCast, Juice, and BubbleUPnP. Some of these programs existed before, but only recently added Chromecast support. Let's go over these programs one by one to understand why Avia is still my #1 recommendation.

•**AllCast** casts music, photos, and video just like Avia, and has a slightly nicer interface. However, it costs $4.99 instead of $2.99, so Avia wins my recommendation.

•**LocalCast** also casts music, photos, and video, and notably, is free. However, you'll have to endure in-app advertisements in exchange for not paying. I have to give Avia the nod, although LocalCast is good if you're on a tight budget.

•**Juice**, like its competitors, casts music, photos, and video and costs only $2.99 like Avia. However, it is a new contender and there are fewer users on support forums to help you if you have a problem. Also, Avia has a track record of consistent updates, whereas it is too soon to know if Juice's developers will provide the same support. Juice could topple Avia in the future, but it needs to prove itself first.

•**BubbleUPnP** also casts music, photos, and video, and costs $4.69. It is a powerful program and has a desktop DLNA server component similar to Plex, but it's not as user-friendly as Avia. If you're a streaming die-hard, you should definitely look into BubbleUPnP, but Avia wins my recommendation because it's cheaper and easier to use for most people.

iOS

There is not yet an all-in-one casting app like Avia for iOS, but iOS users have many more options that they did a couple months ago. Here are the best ways to cast video, photos, and music from your iPhone or iPad.

To cast video saved on your iOS device, your best option right now is RealPlayer Cloud from the App Store. However, it can be frustrating. The app encourages you to upload your video to RealPlayer's cloud servers before playing it, and is picky about what file formats it will play until you do so. Furthermore, it gives you only 2 gigabytes of storage space on the cloud and charges you for additional space. You can give RealPlayer Cloud a shot to see how well it works for you—despite its issues, it's the best option right now—but I expect better options to come out soon.

The most promising alternative on the horizon is PixoCast, which allows casting of videos *and* photos, and is already available for $1.99 from the App Store. It works a lot of the time, but has some bugs— for example, some videos play sideways or upside down. Nevertheless, the developer says a fix is coming soon. When PixoCast irons out these issues, it will be a very good alternative to RealPlayer Cloud.

If you just want to cast photos from your Camera Roll, you can do so with "Photo Cast for Chromecast," available free from the App Store. It also supports slideshows.

There isn't yet a good iOS app for casting music saved on your iPhone or iPad, but there's something nearly as good: you can upload your music to Google Music (p.22) using your PC and cast it using the Google Play Music app from the App Store.

Casting Music and Video from Your Kindle Fire, and How to Cast Amazon Instant Video

Although the Kindle Fire / HD / HDX are Android-powered devices, they are special cases. Unlike most Android devices, the Kindle Fire line of tablets cannot access the Play Store, only the Amazon App Store.

Fortunately, both the Plex Mobile App and Avia are now available on the Amazon App Store. Additionally, many official Chromecast App providers have apps available in the Amazon App Store, including Netflix and Hulu. Most Kindle Fire users report that these apps work well with the Chromecast.

Unfortunately, however, the Kindle Fire does *not* support casting Amazon Instant Video, and there are no workarounds at this time. If you want to cast Amazon Instant Video to your Chromecast, you'll have to do it from your computer using the Amazon Instant Video casting method described below. Hopefully in the future Amazon will enable casting of Instant Video from the Kindle Fire itself.

Amazon Instant Video Casting Trick

To successfully cast Amazon Instant Video from your computer, you need to force Amazon Instant Video to play using Flash instead of Microsoft Silverlight.

To do so, go to Amazon.com, hover over "Your Account," and click "Your Prime Instant Video." Sign in if necessary, and then click "Settings." Select "Adobe Flash Player" and hit Save. Pull up the Amazon Instant Video you wish to watch, and click the play button to watch it using Adobe Flash instead of Silverlight. Cast the tab and then put it in full screen and hide it using the techniques I taught you earlier.

If those steps do not work, you can also try disabling the Silverlight plugin completely. To do so, type "chrome:plugins" into Chrome's search/URL field and press enter. Scroll down until you see "Silverlight," and disable it. Most of the time, this should not be necessary if you've successfully changed your account settings as described above.

Remote Controlling Your Chromecast with your iOS or Android Device

If you start a cast using your iOS or Android device, you can easily pause, play, rewind or fast-forward, and change videos using the same app you used to initiate casting. For example, if you cast from YouTube, you can just open the YouTube app to control the cast, or if you cast from Plex, you can just open Plex.

But let's say that you initiate a cast from your computer and then sit down in front of your HDTV in a different room with only your iOS or Android device in your hand. Is there a way to remote control *that* cast from your iOS or Android device?

The answer is yes, for both operating systems. However, Android users again have a bit of an advantage. (After all, Google makes both the Chromecast and Android. Sorry, iOS users.) There is a free app available in the Play Store called RemoteCast, which allows you to easily remote control any cast playing on your Chromecast. To use it, just open it and tap the Cast icon in the upper-right-hand corner of the screen while a cast is playing. RemoteCast will synchronize with the cast and allow you to control it, even if you started it from a different device. You can also tap the menu key of your Android device while in RemoteCast to bring up shortcuts to casting sources such as YouTube, Netflix, Play Music, and Play Movies.

There is no iOS equivalent of RemoteCast yet. Instead, iOS users will need to use an app like TeamViewer or another remote desktop app, which allows you to view and control your computer's entire screen from your iOS device. This approach, while a very interesting concept and useful for many things aside from controlling your Chromecast, is not quite as nimble as RemoteCast for Android. Still, it is the best option available for iOS users and is free. You can download TeamViewer for your Windows or Mac OS computer at http://www.teamviewer.com/en/index.aspx, and get the iOS counterpart from the Apple App Store.

Casting the Screen of Your iOS or Android Device

The Google Cast extension allows full-screen casting for Windows and Mac OSX computers, but the same is not true for iOS or Android mobile devices.

If you want to cast your mobile device's home screen or non-Chromecast apps on your HDTV, currently your only option is to use a third-party screen mirroring app that shows your mobile device's screen on your computer screen and then cast that using Google Cast's full-screen option. There are a *lot* of caveats involved in this approach, though, so read closely.

Alternatively, there are some methods for mirroring iOS and Android screens on HDTVs that do not actually involve the Chromecast at all. I discuss these in the bonus section below.

Overall, screen casting your iOS or Android device is probably something you'll want to avoid until Google itself releases improved software. I have included this section to at least let you know where things stand and give you a starting point if you must have mobile screen casting, but it's not a easy task. For now, I strongly suggest you stick to official Chromecast Apps and Chromecast-enabled software like Avia when casting from your mobile device.

iOS

For iOS, if your device is *not* jailbroken, your only credible option to cast your screen using your Chromecast is a program called Reflector, which works on Windows and OSX but costs $12.99.
http://www.airsquirrels.com/reflector/

If your device *is* jailbroken, you can accomplish your goal without spending $12.99, but you'll have to be comfortable setting up and configuring a VNC server and client. Specifically, you can download Veency from the Cydia app store and use it in conjunction with the desktop VNC client of your choice. http://cydia.saurik.com/info/veency/

Android

For Android, there are various software packages you can use to mirror your screen on your computer, including AirDroid's screenshot function (available on the Play Store), Droid@Screen (http://droid-at-screen.ribomation.com/), and BBQDroid (http://screen.bbqdroid.org/). The first two are free, while BBQDroid costs $4.49 on the Play Store. However, it may be necessary to try multiple programs to find one that properly works with your device. There are so many different Android devices and operating systems out there that no software developer has been able to come up with a one-size-fits-all program for Android screen mirroring.

Moreover, since all of these approaches rely on Google Cast's full-screen option, you can forget about video or smooth animations. They will be far too choppy. Screen casting using this approach is only good for still content.

There were some rumors that Android 4.4.2 Kit Kat would include screen-mirroring features, but those rumors did not turn out to be true. Fortunately, the developer of AllCast already has a working prototype of an Android screen-casting app. When he releases it to the public, which should be soon, I will update this section.

BONUS — Non-Chromecast Methods of Screen Mirroring

The Chromecast is not the only way to mirror your mobile device's screen on your HDTV.

Many Android devices support a protocol called Miracast for screen mirroring, which works much, much better than the methods described above that use a Chromecast. Despite its name, Miracast has no relationship at all to the Chromecast.

To use Miracast, you'll need a newer Android device and an HDTV that supports Wi-Fi Direct. If you want to give it a shot, search Google or YouTube for "Miracast" plus the name of your device to find a tutorial. Note that on Samsung devices, Miracast is called "AllShare Cast" or "Samsung Link."

If you have an iOS device and you really, really need to cast its screen flawlessly, your best option at this time is, unfortunately, an Apple TV.

Turning on Your HDTV Automatically with HDMI-CEC

Many newer HDTVs support a standard called HDMI-CEC. It sounds complicated, but is very simple in practice, and is supported by the Chromecast. HDMI-CEC allows your HDTV and HDMI-connected devices to send commands to each other, even when one of the devices is powered off.

Remember how I told you to plug in your Chromecast using the wall adapter instead of a USB cord to your HDTV? That was so your Chromecast would always have power, and thus the ability to wake your HDTV.

Depending on the brand of your HDTV, this setting may be called HDMI-CEC in the menu, or it may have a proprietary brand name. Regardless of the name, however, the standard is exactly the same. (Confusing, right?) Common aliases for HDMI-CEC include:

•**Sony**: Bravia Sync/Link

•**LG**: Simplink

•**Panasonic**: Viera Link

•**Samsung**: Anynet+

•**Toshiba**: Regza Link

Make sure that the appropriate HDMI-CEC setting is enabled, whatever name your manufacturer uses for it. Consult your HDTV's instruction manual if necessary. Once you have enabled HDMI-CEC, you can cast to your Chromecast any time, even when your HDTV is turned off, and your Chromecast will automatically power it on and switch to its own input. Convenient!

If you have trouble getting this feature to work, make sure your Chromecast is plugged into your HDTV's primary HDMI input. Some HDTVs only support HDMI-CEC on the primary port.

Optimizing Your Chromecast's Wireless Video Settings to Combat Slowdown and Choppy Playback

If you're experiencing laggy, poor performance with your Chromecast, you might need to tweak its settings. Of course, your first step should be to ensure there aren't any other devices on your network consuming massive amounts of bandwidth (downloading files, streaming video, etc.). If you're confident that isn't the problem, your second step should be power-cycling your router and modem; unplug them both for at least a minute and then plug them back in. If the issue is still not resolved, click on the Google Cast button in Chrome and go to "Options."

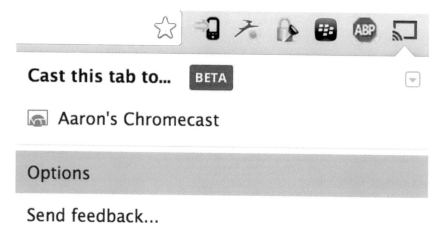

Here, try adjusting "Tab projection quality" down a notch. If it's at "Extreme," set it to "High." If it's at "High," set it to "Standard." This will significantly reduce the amount of data transmitted during the casting process, and will help alleviate any slowdown or buffering you're experiencing.

Tab projection quality

◯ Extreme (720p high bitrate)

⦿ High (720p)

◯ Standard (480p)

If you're unable to solve the problem by changing these settings, I suggest you consult Google's troubleshooting tool: https://support.google.com/chromecast/troubleshooter/2995236

Taking Advantage of Your HDMI Extension Dongle

Another way to combat a poor signal is to plug your Chromecast into the short HDMI extension dongle that comes in the Chromecast's box. The dongle is only a couple inches long, but if the components in your TV are interfering with the Chromecast, those couple inches can be enough to alleviate the problem. This isn't guaranteed to fix your problems, but it's worth a try if you're having trouble.

Using a Travel Router to Make Your Chromecast Work in Hotels

The Chromecast is a natural traveling companion. It's tiny and very lightweight, and is totally free to use, unlike pay-per-view HDTV content found at most hotels and motels. Unfortunately, the Chromecast won't work out-of-the-box on most hotel Wi-Fi networks, because for security reasons hotels do not allow Wi-Fi devices to connect to one another. On a hotel Wi-Fi network, your computer or mobile device will always fail to detect your Chromecast, and you won't be able to cast anything to it. Furthermore, many hotel Wi-Fi networks require you to log in or accept a user agreement, which the Chromecast is incapable of doing.

However, there is a simple and fairly cheap solution: a travel router. You can buy inexpensive, small routers that you can plug into the Ethernet jack in any hotel room to set up your own private Wi-Fi sub-network. Once you set up your network, you can use your laptop or mobile device to bypass any login screens, at which point your devices and Chromecast will be able to interface with each other once again.

Travel routers are readily available on Amazon for about $20, and are all you need to unlock the power of your Chromecast when away from home. They're also incredibly handy for general Internet use, especially if you travel frequently.

I recommend the TP-LINK TL-WR702N Wireless N150 Travel Router ($19.99 on Amazon). If you have an N150, you'll want to use it in WISP + Dynamic IP mode with your Chromecast. See its instruction manual for details. http://www.amazon.com/gp/product/B007PTCFFW

Alternatively, if your smartphone has a wireless hotspot feature, you can use it to set up a Wi-Fi network for your Chromecast. If you take this approach, make sure you have a large data allowance for your tethering plan, or you could run up a big bill.

Casting to Multiple Chromecasts from Your Computer

If you have multiple Chromecasts on your network, you can use your desktop or laptop computer to cast to several of them at the same time.

With each user account set up in Chrome, you can cast one tab, plus up to one video from each Chromecast App. For example, using my Chrome account alone, I could cast YouTube to Chromecast 1, Netflix to Chromecast 2, Hulu to Chromecast 3, and Amazon Instant Video to Chromecast 4 in a tab. And assuming my CPU and Internet connection could keep up, I could cast even more Apps as long as I only cast a single video from each app.

If you want to cast multiple instances of the same app—say, two different YouTube videos to two different Chromecasts, you'll need to create additional Chrome user accounts. You can do this under the "Users" subheading of Chrome's settings page.

Don't get your expectations up too much, though. Unless you have a truly exceptional Internet connection and computer, you'll most likely max out at two or three casts, depending on what exactly you're casting.

Throwing a Raging Chromecast YouTube Party

Okay people; let's not be delusional. No YouTube party will ever qualify as "raging." But you can get as close as possible using YouTube's "TV Queue" feature on iOS and Android.

On your iOS or Android mobile device, open the YouTube app, and before opening a video, tap the Cast icon in the upper-right-hand corner of the screen to connect to your Chromecast. Have your friends do the same. From then on, anytime one of you clicks a video in the YouTube app, there will be an option to play the video instantly or add it to a communal playlist.

So next time you're at a hopping YouTube banger, instead of meekly saying, "Hey, play my video next," make the Alpha move of adding it to the queue along with all your friends' videos. Boom.

If you don't plan to throw a YouTube party, you can also use this feature to make your own YouTube playlist in advance of a marathon viewing session. This can be particularly handy if you're watching a movie with multiple parts.

Using Your Chromecast With a Stereo System

If you have a high-end stereo system, you might want to use your Chromecast to stream audio without involving a television at all. Or, you might want to bypass the audio processor in your TV and connect directly to your receiver. Here are a couple of options.

If you just want a cheap way to stream music and music alone, search eBay for an item called "White HDMI female to VGA Converter Adapter 1080P With Audio Cable For PC TV." It costs about $10 and will convert the Chromecast's audio output into a 3.5mm output. (Leave the VGA output unplugged.)

If you want a higher quality way to split audio off to a receiver, I recommend an HDMI audio extractor. You can pass the Chromecast's connection through one of these boxes to split off audio and video into two separate channels. HDMI audio extractors are readily available for less than $40 on Amazon, and better quality units are available at a higher price.

Of course, if you don't mind the signal traveling through your TV's audio processor, you can just run a cable from your TV's audio output to your receiver and save some money.

Casting a Google Hangouts Video Call, or Using Your Chromecast as a Baby Monitor

Hangouts is Google's video and text communications platform. You can use Hangouts to instant message (IM) back and forth with your contacts or video chat with them face-to-face, like with Skype. If you use Gmail, you're probably already familiar with Hangouts thanks to the Hangouts widget in your Gmail inbox.

Casting a video Hangout can be useful for a few reasons:

•You have too many people trying to crowd around your computer screen

•You're using Hangouts for a business call and you want to project it on a big screen

•You're watching a public Hangout that you're not actively participating in

If you have very young children, you can also use this feature as a baby monitor. Set up a spare laptop in your child's bedroom at night, and cast the video to your television in another room.

You can cast your video Hangout, but there's a special trick to it.

First, go to the following link. https://plus.google.com/u/0/hangouts

Second, click the "Hangouts" button in the upper-right-hand corner of the screen (not the one in the upper-left-hand corner).

Third, click "Start a video Hangout." When the popup window appears, copy the URL of that webpage, paste it into a regular Chrome tab, and hit enter. This step is necessary because the pop-up window does not give you access to the Google Cast button.

Fourth, cast the tab using the tab-casting technique. Presto! Invite other contacts and carry on with your Hangout as usual.

Casting 3D Video to a 3D TV

The Chromecast is fully compatible with 3D video, though you'll obviously need a 3D-capable television to take advantage of this feature. If you have 3D content saved on your computer's hard drive, you can cast it using Plex (p.20). If you just want to give 3D a spin, try the following YouTube channel. http://www.youtube.com/user/3D

Stocking Up on Chromecast-Compatible Android Apps

The Google Play Store has a well-hidden Chromecast section. Don't ask me why Google makes it so hard to find; it doesn't make any sense to me.

To access this treasure trove, open Google Play on your Android device, tap the "Apps" button, and then swipe left to the "Categories" tab. Tap the "Chromecast" button. You'll be taken to a list of Chromecast-compatible apps, such as Netflix, HBO GO, Pandora, and more.

Casting in Incognito Mode

From time to time, you may want to cast a video that you don't want to appear in your browser history. I'm looking at you, Bronies. But by default, the Google Cast extension is unavailable in Chrome's Incognito mode. To work around this limitation, follow these instructions:

• Type **chrome://extensions** into a new Chrome tab and hit Enter

• Look for the Google Cast section and check "Allow in incognito"

• Open a new Incognito window, and cast away without leaving a trace.

Turning Your TV Into a Digital Photo Frame or an Art Exhibit

Have you ever wanted to customize the Chromecast's screensavers? It's now possible to do so with Artkick. This free Android/iOS app gives you two choices. You can either set it to cast famous works of art and stunning photographs from museums, NASA, and the Library of Congress, or you can set it to cast photos from your personal Facebook, Flickr, Instagram, Picasa, or SmugMug account. Artkick uses your Chromecast to turn your TV into a digital photo frame or an art exhibit. Check it out at http://www.artkick.com/, or search for "Artkick" in the Google Play Store/App Store.

Using Your Chromecast to Give PowerPoint Presentations

As I noted earlier in this book, PowerPoint is a natural fit with the Chromecast. If you're in a conference room or a classroom with an HDTV, a Chromecast is a good alternative to a traditional projector.

If you decide to use your Chromecast this way, make sure you're prepared. You'll need to put your Chromecast and laptop on the same Wi-Fi network, which will require re-running the Chromecast setup procedure. From there, you can open your presentation, cast your entire screen, and give a successful presentation. Make sure you test this beforehand, as some corporate Wi-Fi networks may not work with the Chromecast. In a pinch, your phone's hotspot feature will also work.

If your presentation is stored on Google Drive, you can also cast directly from the Drive website:

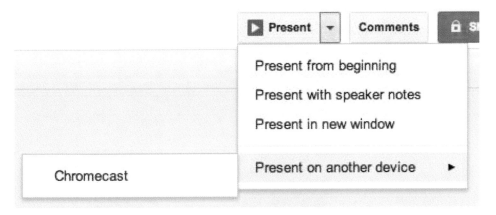

Using an Android or iOS Device

Unfortunately, there are not yet any Android or iOS PowerPoint apps capable of casting to a Chromecast. If you want to give a PowerPoint presentation from your mobile device, the best way to do so is to save your slides as a series of .JPG images and cast them using Avia (Android) or Photo Cast for Android (iOS) (p.24). Of course, this approach does not allow the use of any special effects.

Playing Games on Your Chromecast

There are now some games available for the Chromecast. They're not exactly jaw-dropping (to say the least), but some of my readers have asked about Chromecast games. If you're interested, here are a few to try. You'll need an Android or iOS device to play these.

•**Roll It** (http://g.co/rollit): Open Roll It's page in Chrome, and follow the instructions to start playing.

•**Super Sync Sports** (http://g.co/super): Open Super Sync Sports' page in Chrome, and follow the instructions to start playing.

•**Tic Tac Toe for Chromecast**: Download the mobile app from the Play Store or the App Store and follow its instructions to start playing.

•**Qcast**: Download the mobile app from the Play Store and follow its instructions to start playing. Qcast is only available for Android.

Accessing Advanced Settings - For Power Users Only!

Did you know there are some hidden elements in the Chromecast's Options menu? Open it up:

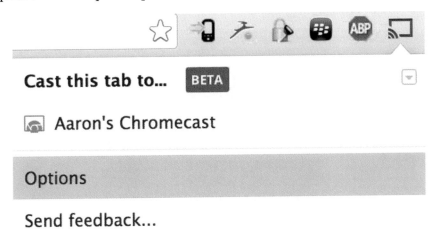

Once in the Options page, right click anywhere in the tab and click "Inspect Element."

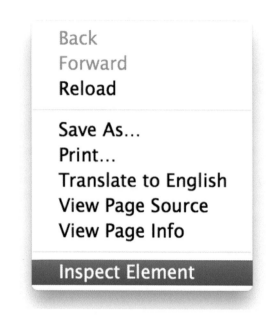

In the large window that appears in the bottom of the screen, you will see a line that contains, among other things, the text **class="options-sections"**. Click on that line to highlight it.

```
m'" class="options-sections" style="display: none;">…</div>
```

Then, in the "Styles" box to the right, uncheck "**display: none;**".

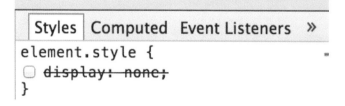

Now, "X" out of the Inspect Elements window and scroll down the page. You will see a new bank of settings entitled "Custom mirroring settings." These settings are not for the faint of heart; don't change them unless you know what you're doing! Mostly, just be aware that they exist, in case you ever need to follow a tutorial involving them.

If you have a Netflix subscription, you can take advantage of a special tool for testing these streaming settings. On Netflix, search for "Example Short 23.976." When you cast it to your Chromecast, it will display your bitrate, resolution, and data transmission speeds, helping you ensure your changes are having the desired effect.

Resetting Your Chromecast to Factory Defaults

It is easy to reset your Chromecast to its factory default settings and wipe its memory of your wireless network settings. You might want to do this if:

•Your Chromecast starts to function erratically

•You decide to sell it

•You want to set it up on another Wi-Fi network

•You just want to start fresh with it

To do so, unplug it from your HDTV but leave its power cable plugged in. Hold the tiny button on the end of the Chromecast for about 30 seconds. The light will begin to blink white, and then turn solid red. When it does, release the button and wait for the light to begin blinking white again. At that point, you can reconnect the Chromecast and start the setup process (p.11) once again.

The Chromecast's LED Statuses

The Chromecast's LED has three states:

•**Blinking white**: Not connected to Wi-Fi and waiting to be configured.

•**Solid white**: Connected to Wi-Fi network, but does not necessarily have Internet access.

•**Solid red**: Rebooting.

Taking it to the Next Level: Rooting and Beyond

By now, we have covered nearly everything you can do with the Chromecast. In closing, let me discuss a few final issues.

Rooting Your Chromecast

You may be familiar with the concept of rooting an Android device; rooting refers to gaining access to the "root" user account, which is the most privileged user account on Unix-based machines. Having root access allows you to run programs you cannot normally run, and do all kinds of fun things. For example, on rooted Androids you can install ad-blocking software, install modifications like call recording software, and more.

Obviously these features don't exist on a Chromecast; the main reason to root your Chromecast is to change its DNS server settings, which is necessary if you travel internationally and want to access region-restricted videos. However, it is only possible to root certain, older Chromecasts that have not received recent software updates. If you got your Chromecast in late 2013 or early 2014, you are probably out of luck, at least for the time being.

If you want to check your Chromecast's vulnerability to rooting, start here: http://forum.xda-developers.com/showthread.php?t=2537022

Upcoming Chromecast Apps

Google just announced a batch of new Chromecast Apps in December 2013, including Vevo and Plex, but you can expect to see even more new Apps in the coming months. Also, Google finally released the Chromecast development kit to software developers in February 2014, resulting in a surge of new third-party apps. This momentum will only increase in the coming months.

Finding More Ways to Use Your Chromecast

This book has already covered the best and most powerful ways to use your Chromecast, but if you want to explore even more options, I suggest starting with this webpage:
http://www.reddit.com/r/Chromecast/comments/1x0cee/chromecast_suppo
rted_apps/

There, you'll find an up-to-date list of Android apps, iOS apps, and other software that works with the Chromecast. If you've read this book, you'll already be familiar with most of the information, but you'll be able to find some new tips and tricks that didn't make it into this book.

For example, you can find information on Vbukit, which allows other people to cast to your Chromecast from outside your Wi-Fi network. Or, you can find more information on Mono, a music-discovery app that supports the Chromecast. You might also be interested in BeyondPod, which lets Android users cast their podcast feeds.

The author of this webpage updates it regularly, so it's a good place to start your own research if you're looking for even more options.

Other Chromecast Resources

With this guide, I have done my best to provide you with a clear and full picture of the things you can do with your Chromecast. However, new uses are being discovered all the time, and it is always possible that you will have unexpected road bumps while setting up your Chromecast or using it. If you have problems with your Chromecast or need help with it, I suggest reading and participating in the following discussion forums. Chances are you'll be able to find a discussion thread about the problem you're having, and if not, you can post one yourself. Of course, let's hope that everything goes smoothly from the beginning.

Google's Official Chromecast Support Forum:
https://productforums.google.com/forum/#!forum/chromecast

Chromecast on Reddit: http://www.reddit.com/r/Chromecast/

Chromecast on Android Central:
http://forums.androidcentral.com/google-chromecast/

Appendix of Updates

I update this book at the beginning of every month. Updates are 100% FREE for life via Kindle. All buyers of the paperback edition can obtain a free Kindle copy through Amazon's MatchBook program. https://www.amazon.com/gp/digital/ep-landing-page?ie=UTF8&*Version*=1&*entries*=0

To find out what's changed since the last edition, check here. It's a lot faster than re-reading the entire book.

March 2014 Edition

Google released the Chromecast development kit to software developers in early February, so there's a lot of new information this month. Here are the highlights for the March 2014 Edition of *Unlock the Power of Your Chromecast*:

•Updated the Plex section. The Plex Mobile App now supports casting music and photos, in addition to video, from an Android or iOS device. Read more here (p.20).

•Added two methods to use Plex with your Chromecast without paying for a Plex Pass. Read more here (p.21).

•Added a discussion of new apps that compete with Avia and RealPlayer Cloud, for both Android and iOS. There was a lot of important activity on this front in February, especially for iOS users. Read more here (p.24).

•Added instructions for casting your music collection using Google Music. Some users may prefer this method to using Sockso, which I suggested in previous editions of this book. Read more here (p.22).

•Added instructions for customizing your Chromecast's screensaver with Artkick. You can choose to display famous paintings and stunning photographs, or you can have Artkick display your own photos. Read more here (p.42).

•Added a section about PowerPoint presentations with Chromecast. Read more here (p.43).

•Added a section about Chromecast games. <u>Read more here</u> (p.44).

•Updated the instructions for casting Amazon Instant Video. <u>Read more here</u> (p.27).

•Updated information about Android screen mirroring. It turns out this feature wasn't included in Android 4.4.2 Kit Kat as expected, but a good solution should arrive soon. <u>Read more here</u> (p.29).

•Expanded the section about HDMI audio extractors to include a broader discussion of using the Chromecast with a stereo system. <u>Read more here</u> (p.37).

•Included more detail in the section about traveling with your Chromecast, including a specific travel router recommendation. <u>Read more here</u> (p.34).

February 2014 Edition

•Added instructions for casting 3D video to 3D-enabled HDTVs

•Added instructions for casting a Google Hangout

•Added instructions for using your Chromecast as a baby monitor

•Added instructions for accessing the Chromecast section of the Google Play Store on Android devices

•Added instructions for casting video in Incognito mode

•Added brief troubleshooting advice to the HDMI-CEC section

•Added the VirtuaWin workaround for full-screen video casting in Windows

•Added instructions for accessing Netflix's Chromecast test video

•Added an additional way of browsing your hard drive for use with the Drag-and-Drop method (using file:///)

•Revised section about casting content saved on Android/iOS mobile devices

•Revised section about casting iOS/Android screens; added bonus section about Miracast

•Removed outdated instructions for casting Plex without a Plex Pass, and revised information regarding the Plex Mobile App

•Removed erroneous information about operating Chromecast with a VPN

•Miscellaneous readability edits throughout

January 2014 Edition

•First edition

Subscribe to this mailing list to receive FREE monthly updates:

http://www.aaronhalbert.com/phplist/?p=subscribe&id=3

Printed in Great Britain
by Amazon.co.uk, Ltd.,
Marston Gate.